The Next Step In Agricultural Education: Or The Place Of Agriculture In Our American System Of Education

Eugene Davenport

In the interest of creating a more extensive selection of rare historical book reprints, we have chosen to reproduce this title even though it may possibly have occasional imperfections such as missing and blurred pages, missing text, poor pictures, markings, dark backgrounds and other reproduction issues beyond our control. Because this work is culturally important, we have made it available as a part of our commitment to protecting, preserving and promoting the world's literature. Thank you for your understanding.

THE NEXT STEP
IN
AGRICULTURAL EDUCATION

OR

THE PLACE OF AGRICULTURE IN OUR AMERICAN SYSTEM OF EDUCATION

AN ADDRESS
BY
E. DAVENPORT
Dean of the College of Agriculture and Director of
the Agricultural Experiment Station,
University of Illinois

URBANA, ILLINOIS

THE NEXT STEP IN AGRICULTURAL EDUCATION
OR
THE PLACE OF AGRICULTURE IN OUR AMERICAN SYSTEM OF EDUCATION

The most significant fact in the educational world to-day is the demand that agriculture be taught in the public schools.

This is a radically new movement in education. Twenty-five years ago—fifteen years ago—it was unheard of. At that time, had the proposition been made, it would have interested neither the farmer nor the educator; the one would have been indifferent, the other would have been horrified or amazed, according as the humor of it might have struck him. To-day it is a live problem in which both the farmer and the educator are seriously interested, and it is one whose solution concerns them both.

Thinking men of all classes are now agreed that in some way and after some fashion agriculture must be taught in our public schools, both primary and secondary; meaning by agriculture not only the occupation of farming, but also the life of the farmer and the genius and spirit of country affairs; for agriculture is not only a profession but it is a mode of life. It is, of course, unnecessary to emphasize the peculiar importance of teaching the fundamental principles and practices necessary to permanent systems of successful agriculture. Other great industries are commonly controlled from central offices, but every farmer must have knowledge sufficient to make him intelligent concerning methods essential to permanent agricultural prosperity.

Now, two radically different methods have been proposed for meeting this new educational demand in the secondary schools. The one method proposes a separate system of schools for country people, to be known as agricultural high schools, farm schools, etc., in which agriculture for boys and domestic science for girls should be the leading subjects taught, assuming that existing high schools in general shall be known and considered as "city schools," whose business it is to minister to the people of the cities and their concerns as the agricultural schools should minister to the affairs of the country. Several of these agricultural high schools have been already established, notably in Wisconsin and Georgia, and a bill which is now in Congress is designed to make the distinction not only clear but permanent, as between agricultural high schools that serve the people and interests of the country, and city high schools that serve the people and interests of the city.

The other method proposes not one system of secondary schools for the country and another for the city, but a single system for both. It proposes, for example, that the present system of high schools should not be denominated "city high schools" with a narrow range of interests, but that they should be so expanded in personnel and equipment, and so enriched in courses, as to minister to the natural interests of their environment, whatever they may be, agricultural, mechanical, commercial, literary, and what not; and that the present ungraded schools in the thinly populated country districts shall be condensed into larger and stronger units, meeting as they are able the educational needs of their communities, and evolving naturally and ultimately into true secondary schools.

The one proposal is logically for as many systems and types of schools as there are distinct interests and lines of instruction; the other is for a single system of education, with highly differentiated courses taught in the same schools. The one proposes to insert itself by main strength into the very heart of our system of secondary education; the other must of necessity develop by gradual process.

This demand has assumed, therefore, serious proportions so far as secondary schools are concerned, and in a very large sense we are at the parting of the ways in this matter. The demand for education in agriculture has come to stay. Indeed, it is but a part of a larger movement for industrial education; meaning by that, education with a view to some form of useful service in the fundamental industries as well as in the so-called learned professions. This demand has not only come to stay, but it has the sympathy and earnest support of the masses of the people and the very large majority of our best educators. The only substantial difference of opinion is as to the best method of procedure, whether by a series of schools of as many distinct types as there are occupations and interests, or by a single system of schools with separate courses. Which shall be adopted as the final American policy of education is a matter before us for discussion—and there is at present no deeper educational problem—and more depends upon what we actually *do now* within the next five years, than it can depend on what we think and say and try to do twenty-five years from now.

This issue is upon philosophies of education so widely different that the choice once made will be final, and the consequences well-nigh irretrievable. I am one who firmly believes that within the next ten years we shall decide for all time whether we shall reap the full fruits of our thoroughly unique educational opportunities in America, or whether we shall needlessly follow in the footsteps of Europe, where social distinctions were established, and the peasant classes fully fixed, long before the modern age of universal education was thought of.

Personally, I do not believe in that philosophy of education which would establish separate schools for the various industries and occupations of life. I greatly prefer that theory of social and industrial development which would establish and maintain a single system of schools wherein the people of all classes should be educated together, distinct courses being framed and conducted for the benefit of each in so far as the interests differ from those of the common mass or of other professions. My reasons for this preference are briefly as follows:

1. Separate schools can never be so good. This is axiomatic for both economic and pedagogic reasons. No school designed to minister to a single class of people and to a single line of interests can ever be so well equipped in the fundamental arts and sciences — in chemistry, biology, physics, history, literature, economics, and the so-called humanities generally — no such school can be so well equipped as can one designed to minister broadly to a variety of interests. Indeed, even if the attempt is made and a wide range of subjects taught, these same subjects will of necessity be studied and taught from a comparatively narrow standpoint. Every teacher knows and every investigator knows that in order to develop a subject well, either for purposes of instruction or of research, it is necessary to establish and maintain a favorable atmosphere for that particular field of mental activity, and this atmosphere is at its best only in the presence of students *interested mainly in that subject;* that is to say, there is no such favorable place in which the farmer may study chemistry as in company with others, not merely of his own kind but of those who believe that chemistry is the greatest thing on earth. There is no such place for the farmer to study history, and to learn to see himself as others see him, as where he studies history in company with those whose chief interest is not in agriculture or in engineering or in teaching, but rather in history itself, by which we study the true significance of world movements of all classes, and come to know things past and present in their true perspective. That is to say, every man ought to be educated in an atmosphere not especially prepared for him and his own kind, but in an atmosphere and an environment much broader than his own interests. In this country, if our democratic institutions are to be preserved, and if our people are to labor together in peace and understanding, all classes must be educated in an atmosphere at least as liberal and as broad as *all* the interests of any single community can make it.

In saying this, I do not overlook the fact that the separate agricultural school has certain distinct advantages. They are the same advantages that are enjoyed by any other industrial school, or even a theological seminary, arising from the comparative simplicity of the educational contract they undertake. It is a fact, of course, that any school founded, manned, and equipped to do a single thing and minister to a single interest gains much in directness by its simplified problem, and by the direct methods it naturally employs. But it loses in breadth and relative values, as has been indicated, and the best proof of it is that none of the separate schools yet founded offer as much even in science as the nearby high schools; and what they achieve is industrial training rather than industrial education — the training of the operative rather than the education of the citizen.

Sir James Bryce tells us that the chief purpose in studying history is to throw light upon our present action and future policies, because in a large sense history does repeat itself. In this connection it is well to remind ourselves that agricultural and mechanical education started in this country in separate colleges. This was necessary because of the attitude of old line colleges of that day concerning industrial education. But that attitude has entirely changed, and to-day these two fundamental industries are strongest, both in instruction and research — not in the separate agricultural and mechanical colleges, but in our greatest universities, where all forms of education are imparted, and where American energy and American citizenship are trained in a cosmopolitan atmosphere. Not only is this true, but the proportion of agricultural students who return to the farm is greater from our universities than from our separate agricultural colleges, to say nothing of the masses of city boys directed countryward.

So I return to my first assertion, viz., that both from the nature of the case and from the experience of the past we may fairly conclude that separate schools are inferior schools; that they lose more in breadth than they gain in directness, and can never rank in real service to that other type which ministers to many interests and gains directness by its distinctly separate courses.

2. Separate schools will tend strongly to peasantize the farmers. To undertake to train the children of farmers

in a system of inferior schools, such as these must inevitably be, with little knowledge of and less regard for the affairs of other people — such an attempt, if it succeeds, will peasantize the farmers in America more rapidly and more certainly than they were peasantized by other causes in Europe generations ago.

To segregate any class of people from the common mass, and to educate it by itself and solely with reference to its own affairs, is to make it narrower and more bigoted generation by generation. It is to substitute training for education and to breed distrust and hatred in the body politic. Knowledge is necessary to a just appreciation of other people and their professions and mode of life; with this only can a man respect his own calling as he ought and love his neighbor as he should. We cannot segregate and make an educational cleavage at the line of occupations except to the common peril.

Reduced to its lowest terms, one of the present propositions is to transfer bodily the European peasant school to American country soil, the inevitable consequences of which are not difficult to foresee.

We may one day need the real trade school in agriculture—the form of instruction that aims at training rather than education; at information rather than development; at mediocrity and below rather than mediocrity and above. This time may come, but it is not here now, and our greatest present need in agriculture is to educate the land-owners rather than their hired operatives; to educate a class of people upon the land that are in every way the equal of their compatriots in the city or anywhere else.

The European peasant belongs to a class whose economic and social status was fixed generations ago by a variety of causes, mostly political; and when the problem of universal education came up for solution there the only way in which the benefits of education could be approximately enjoyed by all the people was to found a system of peasant schools which should secure results with a maximum of manual training and a minimum of mental education. How difficult of achievement was even this step, will be appreciated by any student of Irish industrial history, or by any one who has read Sir Horace Plunkett's "Ireland in the New Century."

When these times come to this country, if they ever do, I fervently hope that by that time our secondary schools will have become so well organized and so broadly equipped as to handle the trade school together with that higher form of industrial education which now engages our attention.

The American farmer is not a peasant. He has never yet been peasantized, and I fervently hope he never will be peasantized. He belongs mostly to the ancient and honorable Puritan stock descended from that great middle class of England that came to this country to establish and maintain, not aristocratic, but democratic institutions. This is the stock that first felled trees, then built churches and school-houses, and prepared to govern themselves and to found a nation and a race whose institutions should rest on the intelligent activity of all the people.

This stock has never been exceeded, not only for hardihood and industry, but for its appreciation of the benefits of higher education and of the better things of life. This people held three things to be cardinal virtues — to labor, to go to church, and to go to school. This is the people that founded Harvard College in the wilderness. It is from stock of this sort that the typical American farmer is descended, and I would see him so trained and so educated as to remain true to his type for all time. This will require a training and an education that cannot be imparted by any form of European peasant school, however modified; but it will require the best that modern human ingenuity can devise. This great need will be met, when it is met if ever, not by old, but by new systems of education, and they must be wrought by ourselves to meet conditions here.

3. To educate the children of different classes separately is to prevent that natural flow of individuals from one profession into another which is in every way desirable both from the public and the private standpoint. If the children of farmers are systematically put into schools where only agriculture is taught, many a good lawyer and many a good

citizen will be spoiled to make an indifferent farmer. Boys do not necessarily inherit the father's profession. In a very large sense their natural faculties come from that common stock of human characters that constitute the heritage of the race, and the individual has a right to an education that is broader than the occupation and the narrow environment in which he was born. True, he should be educated *through* and to a large extent by means of his environment, because that is the compass of his own experience; but if we educate him *within* his environment, we dwarf him in the process, and we do not truly educate him.

Again, many a boy, city born, has the instinct to get back to Nature. He should have at least a fair chance to do so. Because a girl is born in the country is no sign in America that she should be a farmer's wife; nor if she is born in the city is it a sign that she should not. My plea is, in the name of common sense and American citizenship, educate all these people together in one school, with a curriculum varied enough to fit for more than one occupation and more than one mode of life, to the end that a man may follow the occupation of his father or may change it, as he pleases; but whether he follow or whether he change he shall do so intelligently, and for a reason, and in either case he shall have some knowledge of and sympathy for the occupation and the life of his neighbor.

It is said that if you give a bright boy a good education and broad associations, he will leave the farm, and the only way to keep him there is to train him to be *contented* with a humble life. That false theory of education was exploded long ago. Experience has abundantly shown that education does not necessarily result in taking people out of the country except when that education is one-sided and faulty, as witness the graduates from some of our greatest universities. I have no sympathy with the plan of keeping boys on the farm by the blindfolding process.

There was a time, now happily past, when the schools ignored not only agriculture but all industry. Then unthinking teachers advised bright boys and girls to "get an education so they would not have to work." This sort of doctrine found fertile soil in the young of hard-working, self-denying pioneers, and it was not strange that most young men who had much contact with the schools were lost not only to the farm but to industrial life. Then it was that men saw the best of the young crowding into professions already overcrowded, and they noted with sorrow and regret that education served principally to draw men away from the useful callings and to pile them up like salmon in the spawning season where they were not needed or wanted, and where little awaited but their own destruction.

The country is, and always will be, the great breeding-ground for the nation, and the consequence of this insane movement cityward of the choicest men and minds could have had but one final effect—to put the brains in the city and the brawn in the country. It was not strange that under conditions such as these thinking men first denied higher education to their young because of its inevitable consequences, and then came to demand a form of education that should really serve the needs of industrial people as well as those of professional people. In this way arose the separate industrial schools, but later experience has shown that one extreme is as bad as the other — that industrial training without education is but little better than education without industry, and that both will inevitably result in a most unfortunate sorting process; both alike will prevent that natural flow from one profession or mode of life to another, so essential to meet the natural desires of individuals, and to secure that homogeneousness of population with which only institutions such as ours are safe, or even possible.

Though it is true that educators did not lead in the movement for industrial education, it is true that they were quick to see its significance, and to-day it is our greatest educators and our best teachers who are the most earnest disciples of the doctrine that a system of universal education should fit for *all* the needful activities of a highly civilized race, to the neglect of none and to the prejudice of none.

And this is a perfectly stupendous problem. Think of its new complications! In the old days all that was necessary was to maintain whatever schools could win support and teach the things most easily taught without much regard to the consequences. Now in these days of universal education we must teach what the world needs to know for *all* its essential activities, and we must so conduct our schools as not to greatly disturb the economic or social balance of things; so conduct them that the overflow from one occupation or class shall be naturally compensated by a corresponding inflow of equally desirable individuals from others — all of which is necessary if universal education is to be an unmixed blessing.

4. Secondary schools devoted solely to agriculture would of necessity cover so much territory as to require the students to board and room away from home. This for students of the high school age is unthinkable. Every boy and every girl in the early and middle "teens" should sleep every night under the father's roof, and this can be if a community establishes a single school capable of catering to all its needs, and does not insist upon educating one class here and another there, compelling long journeys to get to the right school. A single agricultural school in ten counties, or in five counties, or in one county—think of it!

The problem of secondary education is very largely the problem of the fourteen-year-old, and we should never rest easy till every farmer's boy and girl may go to the *nearest* high school, and there find instruction not only in agriculture but in the other industries and professions which concern the community, and after having lived the day in an atmosphere broader than their own studies go home again at night to dream of what a great thing the world is and to wake with an intelligent appreciation of the place in it which they propose to occupy.

5. Agriculture not only needs contact with other interests, but they need contact with agriculture. Every one who has had experience with the introduction of agriculture into our state universities will bear witness that the benefits of association are mutual.

In the university which I have the honor to serve, our agricultural students not only get a training and a breadth of vision which they could never get in an institution devoted solely to their own interests, but their presence on the campus is of distinct advantage to the other students. Their directness and their practical methods of work are wholesome to the institution, at least they are so declared by the non-agricultural professors and students alike. In every way, as I see it, much is lost and nothing gained by separating the students of different classes and educating them apart, each in the occupation of the father.

Nor would I put all the so-called industries in one class of schools and the professions in another. In a large sense all study is professional, and in a very large sense, indeed, it is also industrial. Some portion of the training of every individual should be industrial, even manual, and another portion of the training of every individual should be distinctly mental, until habits of thought are formed quite *independent of material activity*. For these reasons, which are fundamental, I would not separate industry from any of our schools. I would make it an integral part of every curriculum, its proportion and character depending upon the prospective profession of the individual; but above all I would have the essence of all occupations, or at least of as many as possible, represented in the same school.

My point is, if all these subjects and professional points of view are offered in the same school with more than one avenue into life, then the opportunity is presented for the individual to acquire professional knowledge and skill without becoming narrow as a man. If farmers and lawyers and editors and engineers and artists and merchants are educated separately they will either hate or despise each other, or both; if they are educated together, each will acquire, besides proficiency in his own line, a sympathy for others that comes so easily with that partial knowledge and acquaintance through daily association in the school age, and that comes with so much difficulty in any other way. A farmer at our university is a little different man because law and economics and engineering and Greek are well taught in neighboring buildings, even though he never take one of the courses laid down in the catalogue. The very fact that they are taught, and that he associates with those who do take them — all this has its effect, and in a thousand ways a man absorbs something out of every activity that is going on about him. My point again is that this is the only adequate atmosphere in which to educate an American citizen, whatever his occupation is to be.

6. To establish separate schools for agriculture is to injure the development of existing high schools. These schools are not "city schools" in any proper sense of the term. The great bulk of them are located in small towns and villages in a distinctly rural environment. To denominate all these as "city schools," to be devoted solely to the interests of city people, is as absurd as it is unjust to them. These schools like all others have the natural right to minister to their constituency; but if now agriculture is to be put off into a separate system of schools just because the high schools have not yet taught the subject, then it will be easy, later on, to cleave off another industrial slice, and again another until the remnant that remains will be suited to nobody's need, unworthy alike of the school and the community it was established to serve; and instead of an organized system of effective education we shall have an incongruous medley of separate and independent schools, each serving its little clientele in a narrow way without much regard to the public good — all of which is against the true spirit of universal education.

The American high school is a new institution. It has arisen from our determination to make education truly universal. Now, universal education means that all the people shall be educated, and in such a way that all the activities necessary to a highly civilized race may develop and go forward. Only a small per cent of the people will ever go to college and *the experiment of universal education will be tried out in the field of the secondary schools.* These, more than the colleges, will prove to be the agencies by which the masses of the people will get their training and their trend. For this reason the future welfare of these schools is to be specially safeguarded; but every subject and interest that is taken away from the high school in the present stage of its development lessens by that much its power to serve the community, and by that much it is a menace to its life and efficiency and a check if not a bar to its further development.

7. Separate schools in agriculture will check the extension of high schools into country communities. High schools started first in the cities it is true, but they are making their way rapidly out into the country, a tendency that is to be encouraged, more especially as they are showing a remarkable disposition to respond to their environment. If the interests are not divided it is entirely possible for any community, without going beyond driving limits, to throw all its energies into a school of secondary grade and make it capable of truly reflecting all its varied interests. This has been found impossible where secondary education is primarily under ecclesiastical influence; it will also be found impossible if interests are to be divided and as many separate schools established as there are interests to be served, but if they will stay together and solve their problems as a unit it is possible for every prosperous community to give its young people at their very doors what is to all intents and purposes a college education.

8. It is unnecessary to found separate schools in order that agriculture shall be taught, and well taught. I am enough of a partisan for agriculture to demand what is needed for its development: to advocate, if necessary, separate schools for this purpose, even if they should result in reducing the scope and curtailing forever the full and possible development of the high school. But it is unnecessary to resort to this expedient in these days. It was necessary to do so in an early day because of the indifferent, not to say unfriendly attitude of the schools of the time, all of which were organized and conducted on the classical basis in order to fit for the so-called learned professions. Such schools had little knowledge of and less sympathy for industrial education, and to get a start at all it was inevitable that separate schools should be established to do what existing schools would not in those days undertake.

But conditions are changed. We are living now in a new

age — in an age which recognizes that the highest purpose in education is to get ready to live; that real education is active, not passive; and that its fruitage is service, not personal gratification. We are living in an age which recognizes that all forms of useful activity can be made yet more useful by the knowledge and the graces of education; and that the man himself is bigger than his occupation—bigger than that narrow avenue of public service through which he obtains his livelihood and discharges the ordinary debts to Nature. We have *all* learned this lesson, and by this time we ought to have learned it well. It is true that education for industrial people, and after that education in and for industry, arose from the masses and was forced upon the schools. I do not forget all this, but I beg to call your attention to the fact that that early demand was a selfish one,—a righteous selfishness, it is true, but yet selfish. The masses wanted education for their own purposes, and it caused no little jolt to the educational juggernaut when they proceeded to get it. But when they had time to recover their breath, educators — real educators — began to take stock of the situation, and they have commenced in these days a new policy of education in the world; a policy which if followed out will develop all our resources, both industrial and intellectual; a policy which will take care of your personal needs, and mine, and yet which is as broad as humanity and all its activities. This new policy is working successfully in our great state universities where men of all classes, aims, and prospects are educated together from the standpoint not of private interest but of the public good. The same policy has commenced its work in our secondary schools, and I am anxious above all other considerations that these schools should solve this whole problem for their communities; besides, I know educators well enough to believe that they will earnestly undertake to do it if they are entrusted with the duty, which is also a privilege.

These modern schools must have a fair chance. They are new institutions; they have hardly been in the field a half century, and how they have grown! There are literally hundreds of them that are giving a better education than colleges gave a generation ago, and they have only commenced to serve the people. If they have not yet solved all the problems and taught all the subjects the people need, it is no sign that they cannot or that they will not, and they should be given the chance. Every new addition to an educational institution not only serves a new public need, but it enriches all that was before. All the modern secondary school needs in order to serve us perfectly is men and money, and time to learn how.

There is no longer an "issue" in education — certainly not concerning the fundamental industries. I am told that in certain remote sections of the country some people are still fighting the Civil War, but most of us know that it is over. The old issues are settled and dead and left behind. New ones have arisen to command our attention, and it is unworthy of ourselves to expend our energies on lines of effort long since rendered obsolete.

Yes, the old issues between the classics and the industries are dead and the sooner they are forgotten the better. I have been through this educational conflict myself and I know what it is; but even the old soldier who insists upon fighting the Civil War over again, to-day, will get no audience. New problems have arisen with the new generation, and this generation proposes to stand on whatever has been gained before and expend its energies in forward movements. We do well to imitate its example in this matter. The new issues are constructive.

9. This demand that agriculture be taught in the public schools is but part of the great modern movement for industrial education. Whoever has lived close to the great heart of the common people and has had his hand upon the pulse cannot fail to have felt the throbbings of this new impulse for more than a generation, or to have detected its first feeble flutterings an hundred years ago. And whether he has had his ear to the ground or not, whether he has lived close to the heart of things or away in the upper atmospheres, no man can now be ignorant of the great fact that a change is coming over the spirit of the times regarding educational ideals; a change that is fundamental, and whose shadow or whose light, which-

ever it may be, is full upon us and can no longer be averted or ignored.

When each community had but one or two educated men—the domine, the doctor, and perhaps the lawyer, it did not greatly matter what their education might be like; but when everybody learned to read, and to think, which was inevitable, they quickly saw that the system and the subject matter of an education suited to the office and the study were ill-adapted to fit men for the farm and the shop, but exceedingly well-adapted to unfit them. They, before the educators, learned that the benefits of education were capable of being extended to all the affairs of life, material as well as intellectual.

But, as has been repeatedly noted, educators soon caught the true spirit of the new demand and were quick to respond. They have responded so well as to discover that in the last analysis there is an intellectual basis to all industry and an industrial basis to all education that is safe for everybody to use; they have shown that the names of various occupations are but names for different forms of activity and service; that all fundamental occupations are learned professions, and that any form of education that fits for nothing in particular is worse than useless, even dangerous.

So we must look at this matter broadly. Our problem is but a part of a more general one; moreover, this general problem of how to educate for all the useful activities is the very problem upon which all educators are busily at work, and they are solving it inch by inch and day by day. It is for us to stay with the crowd and be in at the finish.

The American high school is a form of secondary education that has arisen, or more properly speaking is arising, to meet this new demand for universal education. Agriculture, and industrial education generally, have found their true place in the universities. The next step is that they should find their true place in our secondary schools, where, after all, our attempt at universal education will render its greatest service.

And so reasons might be multiplied indefinitely, showing why it is wiser to go forward meeting our educational necessities together — but they would all be of the same general tenor; viz., that our educational problem is after all a single problem — complex, puzzling, and all that; but it is a single problem after all, and we should stay together and solve it.

If the high schools were as indifferent and as antagonistic toward industrial education to-day as the colleges were fifty years ago, I would raise my voice loudest for a separate system of agricultural high schools. But they are not indifferent, they are interested; they are not antagonistic, they are exceedingly friendly. Agriculture has found its place in our American system of education, so far as colleges are concerned, and its place is in most honorable company. It remains to find its place in the high schools, and when that place is found, may it be equally honorable and equally favorable with the place it occupies in our great universities where it has done so well.

And now after having argued, even pleaded for the preservation of the integrity of our system of secondary education, there are two points on which I wish especially not to be misunderstood:

The first one is this: When I speak of teaching agriculture in our high schools, I mean *agriculture*. I do not mean Nature study, nor do I mean that some sort of pedagogical kink should be given to chemistry or botany or even geography and arithmetic. Let these arts and sciences be taught from their own standpoint, with as direct application to as many affairs of real life as possible; but let chemistry continue to be chemistry; let agriculture introduce new matter into the schools and with it a new point of view. Nor should this new matter be "elementary agriculture." In some ways I could wish the phrase had never been coined. What is wanted in our high schools is not elementary agriculture, but elemental, fundamental agriculture. For this purpose we should select out of what is taught in our colleges those phases of agriculture that are adapted to use in the high school and yet that strike at the root of farm life and its affairs—something that will appeal to real farmers and that will serve to actually educate their boys for the business of farming—soil physics, soil fertility, laboratory fields in crop production, the use of farm machinery, and the classification and principles of feeding of live stock.

As I see it, every high school that has a natural agricultural constituency of any considerable importance should put in a department of agriculture on the same basis as its department of chemistry, and proceed to offer at least one year of real technical agriculture taught from the standpoint of the farm, accompanied by such collateral instruction in the arts and sciences as shall provide a suitable course for such of its pupils as find their interests in the country and on the farm.

The other point on which I would be particular is this: I am not arguing that the high schools in their present condition are doing, or are able to do, what is needed for agriculture. My contention is that they can get ready to do it, and that right speedily; and that if they will proceed to get ready, they should have the chance, for it is their opportunity and their privilege; and if they do not propose to serve agriculture and her people as faithfully and as well as they are serving or intend to serve other interests, then they should be compelled to do it. That is my thesis in a few words; but my conviction is that they are for the most part fully ready to turn both their brains and their tremendous efficiency loose on our problem if we will let them.

I am glad to say that we have a perfect understanding on this whole matter in Illinois. The schools are not yet ready to teach agriculture, but they will get ready. I would better say, they are ready but not equipped. We do not yet possess text-books and courses of study, but they are being prepared. We do not yet have competent teachers, but they are coming along and the demand will bring the supply. The schools look directly to the colleges of agriculture to furnish, out of their experience, the most suitable material for these courses and to train the first supply of teachers. This they are fully able to do and I am prone to believe that together we can work out this problem, and in the near future if we are all wise and persistent we can provide as good a home education for the farmer as for other classes of our people.

And now if there should be high schools which prefer to go along in the good old way and not to trouble with the newer educational needs and demands, I have a word to say to them.

What our educational development is to be rests largely with existing schools. They can be quick to catch the spirit of a new order of things educational and enlarge both their conceptions and activities; or the new demands will be met by a new system, to the lasting disadvantage of both parties, as I see it.

We cannot afford to break in two at any point; least of all can existing schools afford to see our educational effort divided. The logic of the situation is all against it. The new ideal is that education should fit for something instead of fitting for nothing, and this ideal will prevail among a practical people like ourselves. Educators can take hold of this natural bent for practical activity and cultivate it until as a people we shall be both efficient and cultivated. If they do not do this the efficiency will develop by itself and we shall all come short of our highest possibilities.

The new demand upon the schools is that they should not only picture life as it was in the past, but also as it is now; that they should assist the student in understanding modern life into which he must plunge, and whose responsibilities he must shortly assume. The student feels the right to demand that some portion of his educational career and some part of his school curriculum should be devoted to making *application* of the wisdom of the ancients and the philosophy of life to the conditions of modern existence.

Reduced to the lowest terms and pushed to the last analysis, that is all this new movement means in any of its forms—agricultural or other; viz., that the school hold up a true picture of life in all its activities, and that teaching be conducted from the standpoint of living, not merely of mental development; that the school shall be a true mirror of human life, modern as well as ancient, and of what men do as well as of what they think and say. In other words, that a system of universal education shall universally educate,—not in art without industry; not in industry without art, but in both art and industry so joined as to make possible the highest civilization and the greatest development of which the human race is capable. To this end may agriculture, like every other form of useful activity, find its place in our existing system of education, and may that place be one that comports with the importance of the profession, the mode of living of its followers, and the philosophy of life on which our great social structure rests; for after all, the greatest thing in the world is to live a full and perfect life.

Sixty years ago Professor Turner wrote: "All civilized society is, necessarily, divided into two distinct co-operative, not antagonistic, classes:—a small class, whose proper business it is to teach the true principles of religion, law, medicine, science, art, and literature; and a much larger class who are engaged in some form of labor, in agriculture, commerce, and the arts. For the sake of convenience, we will designate the former the Professional, and the latter the Industrial class; not implying that each may not be equally industrious; the one in their intellectual, the other in their industrial pursuits. Probably in no case would society ever need more than five men out of one hundred in the professional class, leaving ninety-five in every hundred in the industrial; and, so long as so many of our ordinary teachers and public men are taken from the industrial class, as there are at present, and probably will be for generations to come, we do not really need over one professional man for every hundred, leaving ninety-nine in the industrial class.

"The vast difference, in the practical means, of an appropriate liberal education, suited to their wants and their destiny, which these two classes enjoy, and ever have enjoyed the world over, must have arrested the attention of every thinking man. True, the same general abstract science exists in the world for both classes alike, but the means of bringing this abstract truth into effectual contact with the daily business and pursuits of the one class does exist, while in the other case it does not exist and never can till it is new created.

"The one class have schools, seminaries, colleges, universities, apparatus, professors, and multitudinous appliances for educating and training them for months and years, for the peculiar profession which is to be the business of their life;

and they have already created, each class for its own use, a vast and voluminous literature, that would well nigh sink a whole navy of ships.

"But where are the universities, the apparatus, the professors, and the literature, specifically adapted to any one of the industrial classes? Echo answers where? In other words, society has become, long since, wise enough to know that its teachers need to be educated, but it has not become wise enough to know that its workers need education just as much."

Professor Turner was pleading for an Industrial University to serve the educational needs of the 95 per cent as those of the 5 per cent were served by the then existing colleges.

His "dream" is realized and more than realized. In every state there is now at least one institution of college grade ministering directly to these higher needs of industrial life. And what a change they have wrought in the few years of their activity! How the industries of life are developing under the benign and stimulating influence of higher education and systematic thought. How the people themselves are improving as their occupations develop and take honorable place among men!

All this has come about. But since Professor Turner wrote the words I have quoted, an entirely new system of schools has sprung up all over the country—a kind of schools unknown in his day and which does not exist elsewhere than in America.

I refer, of course, to the high school. Equipped as it is to give what is in effect a college education, this institution of the people is the most powerful modern agency for shaping American life. The high schools of the country touch all the people of all classes, and their influence is beyond computation.

And now, I ask the final question: Is this new system of schools to serve only Professor Turner's 5 per cent as did the old time college, or are they to serve the full 100 per cent? Are the high schools to serve the people on the same broad plan of modern colleges, or are they to restrict their attention and their service to the few favored occupations?

These great schools can serve all classes and all interests if they will. It is merely a question of organization. Do I hear the objection that their courses are full—then I will say, make others. Do we have no material? The material lies all about us, in the present-day activities of men and in the great body of scientific truth that is rapidly accumulating. Are our teachers unprepared? Then let them prepare themselves; for as sure as time passes, this matter is upon us, and this question will press for its solution.

If the existing high schools cannot or will not serve the interests of agriculture and her people, then just as certain as the sun rises and sets, a system of schools will be founded that will do it. The farmers of this country are bent on good secondary education that will fit for country life, and if they are obliged to found a new system of schools to get it, then they will do that and insist upon a fair division of the revenues.

Let me be not misunderstood. It is not upon an endowed institution to teach agriculture, unless it chooses to do so; unless it sees in the subject large educative possibilities within the chosen line of its activities and for which it is endowed.

It is different with the high school. This is a public school, supported by public funds, and its obligation is to serve the public well in all its interests—to put its service on the same plan as that of the state colleges and universities, and the temper of the public mind is such as to force the issue, if necessary. If it becomes necessary to found a separate system of schools to do this work it will be the worse for all of us and the better for none. If we go on together and our high schools serve agriculture and her people as faithfully and as well as they serve others, then all will be well.

This then is the place of agriculture in our scheme of education — that it shall become an integral part of our educational system, to the end that all great interests shall be served equally well by a single comprehensive system of schools; and the next step is to see to it that agriculture shall attain the same important and honorable place in our high schools that it has already attained in our universities.

Printed by Libri Plureos GmbH in Hamburg,
Germany